FROM WISHFUL THINKING TO TRUE TRANSFORMATION

7 DAYS TO A NEW YOU

James Patrick Holden

From Wishful Thinking To True Transformation: 7 Days To A New You

Copyright © 2024 by James Patrick Holden

DEDICATION

This book is dedicated to my wife Claire, children William and Mary, and family without whom I would not have had the direction and focus to live into the making of a new reality. It turns out that the inner transformation we all seek is reflected back to us in the relationships with those we love as we pour our best example of our transformation into them. I would be remiss to leave out the recognition of those in life who have also at times reflected back to me my worst example of my lack of transformation as they have equally impacted my direction and focus.

But somewhere very early in my life I became aware of an inner expanse. I knew I could feel something way bigger than me, and it was wonderful. So as the notion of dedication has arisen, I have come to the same idea as I have for as long as I can remember. I dedicate my life and this work to the expanse that draws me back more now so than ever. Before I could name it, I knew it. Now that I could name it any one of the thousand names given it over the last thousands of years, I return to it without a name for it and without a name for me. So in the end or maybe from the beginning I dedicate it all to all of us who already know, or are about to discover the timeless reality.

TABLE OF CONTENTS

FOREWORD

The first writer I watched hard at work was my husband, James. I have never seen such dedication and need to get up so early since his Roofing Contractor exam. Except this time, the passion was to meditate and to get to his writing. The task was familiar to him since he was a pastor for 14 years. On the other hand, I not so much. But the early morning for me was not only to support my husband but to grow in my meditative life.

Writing is hard. I imagine even career authors find that what they thought would be flowing and clear is a tangled mess of jumbled thought, but they manage to put it all together in the end. I am proud of you James. You are amazing in my eyes!

PREFACE

Inspired books seem to write themselves. And the timeless books come from the pens of the still. Finding that place for myself was key. In the early hours then, dedication simply became getting out of bed. Then it became seeing something so completed that the sense of satisfaction usually meant for the end came to inhabit my present moment. So, with a sense of completeness and satisfaction I rolled out of bed day after day to seek out a sense of stillness that as it turns out was not outside of life, but at the center of it all.

The photos are a reminder of the potential the morning has in its beauty and presence.

Thanks go out to Will for the photos on pg. 14,18,20, and 26, and for Mary's on pg. 24.

INTRODUCTION

A direction for daily return to the timeless source of our deepest truths is the purpose of this book. Through poetic form the truths of who we are at our most simple sense of awareness can, if we allow them, free us from old self-perpetuating beliefs. As humanity grows in our understanding of our conscious awareness of ourselves as self-awareness, we are forced to, or freed to, see the impact of the power of our beliefs to create not only our responses to our circumstances in life, but our very circumstances by beginning to embody a new way to understand our life. An understanding where we can see that it is not so much that our lives inform our conscious beliefs of a fixed reality, but our beliefs and our visions of life built on those beliefs inform and create the form of our life and circumstances.

The daily return first thing in the morning creates the pathway, not just in the pattern of life, but in our brains as neural pathways that are built to support our new understanding of reality[1]. The goal is that we find our highest sense of the divine at our center. That in the freedom of letting go we are freed to look upon the stage our form parades us and write the next act with the deepest truths we embrace and see through. Over and over then we answer the question, "What would life look like if we woke up tomorrow and all of the problems of life were gone[2]?" How much more would you paint the new vision if you knew you were first already eternal.

---

[1] Dr Joe Dispenza – Becoming Supernatural: 2017 Hay House
[2] https://positivepsychology.com/miracle-question/

MORNING ONE

The morning dawns, and like the first yawns,
I take in the remembrance of my in-sense.
And as the world falls to the deep my soul calls,
As conditions unravel and free me.
And as I look upon below,
The life my form parades me,
I see the love of a finished day,
And let it fully pervade me.
And without condition, one love for all,
The same for them so as me.
And let fall the best,
For all the rest,
That they may too know what has freed me.

Love

As you begin today, how does embracing a sense of love without conditions change the way you see the outcome of your day?

When you think of the same love for others as for yourself how does that change your thoughts of others?

MORNING TWO

Oh the delight, Oh the Joy!
It is true what they said.
After all of the looking,
After all my heart said,
I have found in my waking,
My inward reflections,
My old thoughts are dead,
My old ways my rejection.
It's new and it's fresh,
There's no more forlorning,
The truth is in me,
Joy comes in the morning!

Joy

How often have you allowed that still small voice to draw you in?

Are you able to let it remind you of the truth that joy is a natural state?

MORNING THREE

Somewhere I dreamt of peace.

Not in a far-off place, but closer.

It was there in the distance, and it was so near.

Even as peace was in my heart,

Peace was closer still.

Each circumstance was a reflection of it.

Answers had been found.

The right action had arisen in the right moment.

And as nothing had been done,

Nothing of the day had been left undone.

For in the satisfaction of its completeness,

In the stillness where I could see it all,

I knew, in letting go,

The peace I had found,

Was the peace that was in me,

Even more than that,

It was me.

Peace

How would the evening feel if the day had been spent mindful of a sense of peace so deep nothing could disrupt it?

MORNING FOUR

This morning I sit in a place,

Where no walls and no time can move me.

I see the world and its ways,

Do we go, do we stay,

But here only I need approve me.

It seems then I have found a gate,

Where completeness entirely finds me.

No want, for perfection is stillness,

No lack, for this patience completes me.

Patience

How can stillness in your life free you from the situations and deadlines that arise in your day?

What would taking a higher perspective of your life, as if watching it play out as an interested observer, do to change or improve your patience with the situations or people you observe?

There is freedom in not needing others' approval. How does patience free you?

Imagine the end of your day having held patience throughout. Can you put on the feeling of completeness and wholeness wanting nothing?

MORNING FIVE

I feel kindness this morning,
For myself from myself.
I feel kindness this morning,
A gentleness of self.
And as gratitude
By relief kindness inspired,
With wholeness by mercy,
In transformation rewired.
And as I offer myself,
Love without conditions,
True freedom from all,
The Divine my connection.
And as I feel the Divine,
Now well up from within me,
With nothing to cling to,
Live presence surrounds me.
I'm reminded of freedom,
I had way back when,
Never lost, now remembered,
That I've always been.

Kindness

How would your day change if you carried the truth that you are choosing today to be kind to yourself?

This idea of being kind to yourself brings up an important part of our lives that we always have ourselves first to consider. We can lift our own sense of the entire day when we choose to show ourselves kindness.

Consider then taking time this morning to paint a vision of the day's end and as you do sense and feel now what it has been like to sense kindness from yourself. Our highest sense of self at our core, where time and space, situations, and experiences fade as they are let go, already knows the truth we seek. That we are already whole and that we are the one offering ourselves kindness.

As we come to see that we are best when we are our own caregiver, what act of kindness would you have for yourself that would help you free yourself from all?

Kindness is freeing for others and for ourselves. What we believe about ourselves either helps or hinders our transformation.

Have you sensed gratitude for the relief that offering yourself kindness brings?

What do you believe about yourself?

Do you believe in your own eternalness?

Have you considered the notion that you are already eternal?

As you spend time in the center of the stillness and it is revealed to you that your sense of freedom, completeness, and wholeness rise with your awareness of your own timelessness, your own eternalness, kindness becomes the offering to a world already searching for the truth you have found.

MORNING SIX

Be gentle this morning,
Did you know that I break?
Without redirection too much hardship I take.
Let's make our way easy,
Let's envision our future,
We can see it completed,
We can fix it with suture.
A sowing of grace in a bit of a bramble,
Belief in our best is this new truth's preamble.
And as the day ends,
It is just as I'd seen it,
My belief in my best,
This whole day redeemed it.

Gentleness

Gentleness is like water. It has no problem with taking the roundabout way. Its resourcefulness has no limits. It is content with the lowest places while ever keeping its completeness.

How do thoughtfulness and gentleness connect for you?
Have you thought to envision your future in such an intentional way?

MORNING SEVEN

Do I really want this much control?
To wake up in the morning foal,
And see my day well ended?
To believe the feelings once for then,
For now embraced, I have befriended.
That I said I would do this,
That I would paint my own picture,
I would fill it with senses,
Its completeness a fixture.
The Divine casts a picture of my lifetime
Just like this.
My perfection as promised,
My eternal witness.
So as much as I think,
Someone else could take over,
I would miss out on my chance,
Of my own visions discover.
And now that I know,
It is as you believe,
My spirit in spirit,
My world does conceive.

For control of myself,
Is in how I choose vision,
Eternal truth is my choice,
My only provision.

Self-Control

So often we are forced to look upon self-control as a negative request by another. It's usually offered after some moment when another might say we "lost" control.

But what if after realizing that we do want and in fact already have control in our lives, we begin to see this self-control idea from a higher perspective?

How would your day play out differently if you embraced your ability to envision the end of your day, week, month, year, life?

What would you want control over in that vision? Would envisioning positive outcomes playing out or grace filled perspectives change your approach to your day?

How would your spirit feel if you knew you wanted to have the sense of peace at the end of your day?

Can you sit still and center yourself while you play out the feeling of peace within, and actually feel relief, contentment, and completeness knowing it will come at the end as you sense it now?

THOUGHTS

Feel the physical feeling,
You feel you need to feel.
For feeling is a finite fact,
A fact for sure that's real.
If lack of feeling finds you foul,
For few so true it is,
Just find the feel,
That is what's real,
To bring back the feeling's fizz.
Find furlough far from frowning faces,
For finding feel sometimes is funny,
For it's the feel that is what's real,
And what you want is feel,
Not money.

Feeling

How does putting on the feeling of already having something change the way you experience desire?

If knowing that all things come to you as you believe, how much more could your life change if you spent time envisioning the feelings associated with your desired changes?

MEDITATION

To all who know a mother's love,
Rejoice in what you reap.
For truth is love's domain inside,
Her heart her soul does keep.
To all who know a mother's love,
Know nothing can compare,
To those who find the simple truth,
In her words I care.
To all who know a mother's love,
Consider then a pause,
To fill the void left from birth,
Serves a higher cause.
So enter love,
And give to her,
A mighty chorus from above,
And give the gift she gave to you,
Return your mother's love.

A Mother's love